ENDEAVOUR MEASUREMENTS

Overall length: 33.3m (109' 3")
Length of lower deck: 29.77m (97' 5")
Breadth: 8.89m (29' 2")
Depth in hold: 3.45m (11' 4")
Carrying capacity (burthen): 397
gross registered tonnes
Displaced volume: 550 tonnes
Sail area: 926 sp. m
Masts: Main mast 39m (127' 11")
high, foremast 33.5m (109' 10")
and mizzen 24m (78' 9")

The replica cost $17A million
and took nearly 500,000
man-hours to build

GW01418267

The idea to build a replica of Captain James Cook's famous ship HM Bark Endeavour was conceived in the 1960's in Whitby, England, the port where the original vessel had been built in 1764. In spite of considerable support the project stalled. A second attempt ten years later during the James Cook Bicentennial celebrations in Sydney, Australia also failed. However when the Australian Government decided to build a national maritime museum on the shores of Sydney Harbour to mark the 1988 Bicentennial of European settlement in Australia, opportunity and enthusiasm came together.

The trustees of the new Australian National Maritime Museum took up the challenge to build a replica of HM Bark Endeavour. Bond Corporation of Australia offered to take on the project as a bicentennial gift to the Australian people, and a specially designed shipyard with a gallery overlooking the building dock was erected in Fremantle Western Australia. Work began in January 1988 and the keel was laid in October of that year. Two years later Bond Corporation could no longer support the project and Yoshiya Corporation of Japan offered to complete the ship. However five months later Yoshiya too had to withdraw.

Eventually in August 1991, HM Bark Endeavour Foundation was established in Sydney under the Chairmanship of Mr Arthur Weller CBE, with the support of the National Maritime Museum, Greenwich.

Building recommenced on 26 August, the date that the original ship had sailed from Plymouth 223 years before. Four years later Endeavour was commissioned on 16 April 1994.

This is the story of two ships - James Cook's Endeavour and her 20th century replica. Two Endeavours spanning two centuries, but sharing a common spirit of discovery and adventure.

COVER: *At sea in the Indian Ocean en route to England 1997*
left: *Endeavour running before the wind with stunsails set, Fremantle May 96.*

WHAT IS A REPLICA?

The task of building any replica from a bygone age raises many questions. What was the original like; can we find tradesmen and women with the requisite skills; can we obtain the materials; how much will it all cost; how long will it take? When the replica in question is a 550 ton, 18th century wooden sailing ship that needs to be fully operational in a 20th century world, the questions can seem insurmountable.

The first question for the Fremantle project team was "What is a replica?" Some argued that to be a true replica, the ship had to be built from exactly the same materials as the original, using the same tools and with no additions nor alterations. This was a noble position to take but one which would create tremendous financial, maintenance and safety problems for the future.

A compromise was found and the following criteria were agreed: The ship would be exhaustively researched for historical accuracy. Materials would be chosen for the greatest longevity, but would not be allowed to compromise the original method of construction, nor the spirit of the ship. Modern tools would be used when required.

A minimum of modern equipment would be installed for safe navigation and the health of the crew. With these criteria in place it was time to build Endeavour.

Building begins

Research showed that the original vessel was built of oak, with an elm keel and most likely Baltic pine for her decks, topsides, masts and spars. Oak is very susceptible to rot and to attack from marine borers, particularly in tropical waters. The original ship had survived only 29 years, whereas the replica would have to sail for 40-odd years. Here was our next problem - none of these woods were available in the sizes required, nor at a cost that could be met. We decided to use local wood - the West Australian hardwood jarrah replaced oak, Douglas fir or oregon replaced the Baltic pine. Several other woods were used including karri, wandoo, blackbutt, tallow wood and tuart, with sheoak for the blocks.

right: *The hull takes shape clearly showing the huge laminated ribs, August 89;* middle: A *traditional adze is used to shape the timbers;* above: *The exterior shutter plank is fitted December 1991.*

bottom left: *Shipwrights man-haul timber from the state forest;*
top left: *Blacksmiths working on the metal fittings for the ship;*
middle bottom: *The weather deck takes shape, November 92;* **middle top:** *Driving home the traditional wooden nails (trunnels);* **right:** *Carving the ornate quarter window badges.*

Some timber was specifically cut for the ship, however we purchased recycled wood whenever possible, from a redundant timber bridge, an old wheatbin, a war-time munitions factory, a woolstore and even a disused nunnery! Huge pieces of timber which had been felled during road construction work, were cut into supporting knees, together with wood from the state forests which, due to a ban on vehicles and animals in the area, had to be dragged out by our shipwright's sheer muscle power.

It was impossible to find the huge timbers needed for the early construction stage and these had to be laminated. One inch jarrah boards were stacked together, cut to the required shape, taken apart and then glued back together; it was rather like doing a gigantic three dimensional jig-saw puzzle. All of the laminated wood was eventually covered with planking. To be faithful to the original construction the floors and bends were made separately and fastened together with chocks. As the ship progressed less lamination was needed, and the recycled materials were used for the breast hooks and deck fittings. All the external planking is solid timber, except the large curved wale around the bow and the planking immediately above.

The original method of fastening was by large iron bolts ron rod rivetted over plates at each end). We copied this ethod, but to make them longer lasting we galvanised and readed them on one end only, to obtain a really tight joint. n places where threaded rod would show, copper rod was vetted over clench plates.

All planking was fastened in the traditional manner using ousands of trunnels (wooden nails). However below the aterline and at the ends of the planks coach bolts were used stead of iron spikes for added security. As each piece of timber as shaped it was treated first with an epoxy based preservative nd finally red lead.

The traditional skills of the blacksmith and the wood carver ere used extensively throughout the ship.

A blacksmithing shop was built at the Fremantle yard and l the iron fittings including bolts, spikes, plates, mast straps, on bound blocks, door hinges, hooks, the two stoves, the stern ntern and over 30 hanging lanterns were reproduced.

The original ship featured a considerable amount of ecorative carving. Designs for these were based on original plans and a drawing by one of the artists who sailed with Cook. All carving was done by hand, and finished ashore before fitting to the ship. The reason for the carved sailor's heads on the carrick bits is not known; perhaps they were to show what a real 18th sailor looked like!

The modern paints and varnishes used to protect the hull, were matched to original 18th century colours indicated by the research programme.

In 1768 HM Bark Endeavour carried five boats, a longboat, pinnace, yawl and two small skiffs, one for the boatswain, the other belonging to Joseph Banks. These were usually stowed inside one another on the boat booms, while the heavier longboat was probably kept on top of the main hatch. As the replica is required to carry modern rescue craft, we do not have the space to include these boats; however we have built the original pinnace which is on show at the National Maritime Museum in Sydney.

The final structure of Endeavour is immensely strong. Stronger than the original. Yet at sea, she moves and creaks and groans as surely as James Cook's Endeavour.

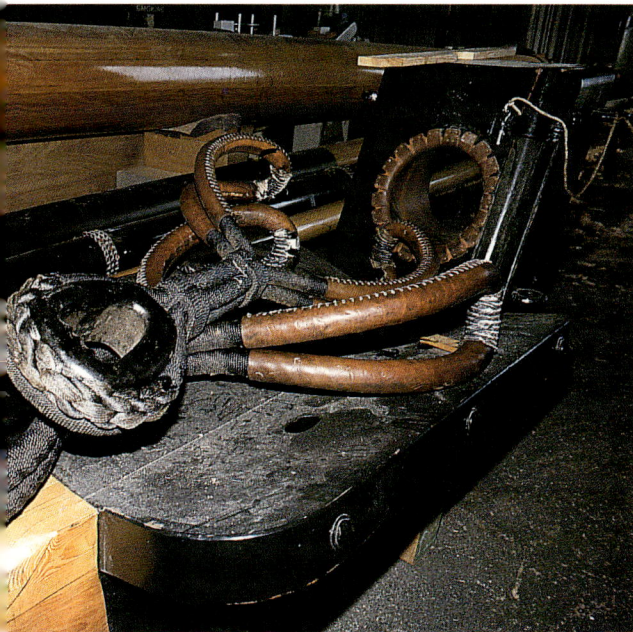

RIGGING & SAILING ENDEAVOUR

When the Admiralty purchased Endeavour in 1768, although she was only three years old, they found all her spars rotten and in need of re-rigging. Spars are all the ship's masts, yards, booms, gaffs etc. Deptford Yard drew survey drafts of the ship and noted the dimension of these original spars. Again this posed a question - were these the actual lengths of the spars or the length of the valuable timber remaining in the spars? The usual practice of the time was to leave out the damaged or rotten wood from the surveyed length. Was this the case here?

With no contemporary rigging and sail plan available, we consulted various 18th century references and after much wrangling and discussion, the final dimensions and rig for the replica was decided.

Endeavour is ship rigged, carrying square sails on all three masts, t'gallant, topsails and courses on the fore and main mast, and topsail and fore and aft course or 'driver' on the mizzen. A massive bowsprit projects from her bow, and supports a lighter jib boom. Below these hang the spritsail and spritsail topsail, which to our 20th century eyes look so odd, but in practice have proved to be very effective.

In between these square sails are a large number of fore and aft stay sails permanently hanked to their appropriate stays. Finally projecting from the main and topsail yards and the channels, stunsails can be rigged which greatly increase the sail area in light to moderate breezes.

Having decided on the lengths of the spars, the next step was to build them.

In the eighteenth century the smaller masts and yards were shaped from single pieces of solid timber. The lower masts

were 'built' using solid pieces of timber held together by lashings called 'woldings'. The structure supporting the large platforms or 'tops' was attached to the masts with a series of bolts, iron bars rivetted over clench plates at each end. Again we decided to follow this method of construction and ordered solid Oregon pine from America for the spars.

The Oregon arrived straight from the cold of a Northern hemisphere winter into the heat of a Western Australian summer with disastrous results. The timber soon developed large cracks that made it useless for the masts. It became obvious that large spars built from solid timber would have a fairly short life, and to overcome this baulks of laminated timber were made to replace them.

Only the lightest masts and yards were made from solid timber. The finished spars have proven very reliable and the ship has broken only one spritsail yard and a driver gaff in two and a half years of sailing some of the world's toughest waters.

Rigging

The ship's rigging is divided into two main areas - standing and running. Standing rigging supports the masts and yards, and includes all the ropes that do not move. Running rigging includes all the ropes that move during the setting of sails.

The project team wanted the ropes to look original, which meant we needed four-strand cable laid hemp rope. How could we make this? Happily Australia's leading rope manufacturer, Kinnears, came to our aid. They owned one of the few remaining operational rope walks in the world, and after restoring the 19th century machinery, they were set to make all the cordage we needed. Having solved the 'how', the next problem was to find a substitute fibre as hemp was no longer available. The only alternative natural fibre was manila. This however had the problem of enormous initial stretch, and a tendency to reject

the Stockholm tar coating that was essential to waterproof and prevent the ropes from rotting. The man-made fibres, polyester and polypropylene, were considered as they were easy to maintain and had a long life.

Before making any decisions, the design team developed mathematical models of the rig and tested the various fibres, which proved a lifesaving move. The results showed that if we had rigged using the man-made fibres for the long shrouds and stays supporting the masts, they would have failed in strong weather and caused a disaster. After further study all three fibres were used - polyester for the short, labour intensive strops, polypropylene for the running rigging, and manila for the long sections of standing rigging and the lanyards between the deadeyes and hearts. The manila rope was pre-stretched by weighting with blocks of concrete, and hanging it from a large construction crane.

In the meantime Endeavour's rigging team had patiently taught themselves the 18th century rigging skills they would need, and now set to work.

The rigging also needed over 700 wooden blocks and numerous deadeyes, belaying pins, hearts and cleats. A separate team was formed to make and carve these, while the blacksmith wrought countless bolts, rings, ring bolts, plates, hooks and various other fittings required. Finally the whole rig, mast by mast, was put together in a specially constructed jig outside the main shipyard. When the Endeavour was launched, the rigging was ready to install.

The 18th century sails were made of flax, however we decided to use a Scottish man-made material called Duradon. This material looks and feels very much like flax, and is lighter to handle and resistant to rot. Fortunately it also gets dirty easily so it would not be long before the sails would loose their newness. Due to the immense size and number of sails required it was decided to machine-sew the fore and main mast sails, while the sails for the mizzen mast were hand-sewn. This would enable their relative performance at sea to be gauged. The use of a modern sewing machine represents a very small part of the work on Endeavour's sails, as all the bolt ropes, reefing points, clews etc were worked into the sails by hand.

Sailing

Unlike other replica ships, many of which have scaled-down rigs for ease of handling, Endeavour's rig is exactly the same size as the original. The question of how she would sail was one we constantly asked during the six years of construction. In retrospect we need never have concerned ourselves with this question. The Endeavour is a thoroughbred, her design having evolved over many years of sailing the treacherous North Sea. From the first day we sailed she was sea kindly, dry, easily driven, forgiving and surprisingly fast. In ideal conditions, 25-30 knots aft of beam, Endeavour sails in excess of 9 knots, and she tacks through about 160 degrees. After returning to England, Cook stated in a report to the Admiralty that in ideal conditions HM Bark Endeavour would do 7 to 8 knots. Why the difference in speeds?

Our project team researched the amount of sail Cook carried in various wind conditions. It took imagination to interpret "ligh

top left: *A crewman climbs the ratlines on the forward mast beside the carved heads on the windlass;* top: *Crew on the huge bowsprit prepare to handle the spritsail;* top inset: *A few of the 700 wooden rigging blocks;* bottom: *Precariously balanced a crewman frees a bunt line on the main sail.*

irs, fresh breezes, moderate gales" into wind speed measured in nots, but they found that Cook generally carried less sail than he replica. Obviously he was protecting his sails and masts which ad to last the 3 years, and probably he was obeying the Admiralty rder not to press the ship unless giving chase or being chased. Ve can only assume that we sail faster due to the smoother nature f our underwater surface, and because Cook generally carried ess sail than we do.

The Endeavour family

Endeavour is manned by a professional paid crew of 13, including the Captain, together with a voyage crew of up to 40 volunteers. Voyage crew are recruited from the countries the ship visits. They need to have some maritime experience and be physically capable of crewing what is fundamentally a primitive vessel.

Although only 56 people sail on Endeavour at any one time, she is supported by a large group of people from all over the world: the 100 men and women who built her; 2000 odd volunteer guides, trained and outfitted in her ports of call, who look after the museum displays; the dozens of volunteer workers who cheerfully clean, paint and polish; the individuals and companies who freely give of funding and their expertise.

This is the Endeavour family, the true custodians of the ship's spirit and evolving traditions.

HIS MAJESTY'S BARK ENDEAVOUR

It was early November 1768, and His Majesty's Bark Endeavour was anchored in the bay of Rio de Janeiro, Brazil. Her captain, Lieutenant James Cook walked angrily up and down the quarter deck. How dare the Viceroy Don Antonio Rolim de Moura seize the longboat and throw his men into jail? How dare he refuse anyone from the ship, including Cook himself, to step ashore unless under armed guard? Why would he not believe the truth, that Endeavour was on a scientific voyage of discovery in the name of the King of England and the Royal Society of London, to view the Transit of Venus and look for new lands, new people, new flora and fauna? Perhaps the answer lay partly in Endeavour herself and the Viceroy could be forgiven for thinking that although flying the English flag, she looked more like a merchant ship - for that was exactly what she was - a sturdy little collier built to shift coal around the coast of Britain. What was she doing in Rio?

The Royal Society of London, dedicated for more than one hundred years to scientific study, decided in 1767 to observe the transit of the planet Venus across the sun which was due two years later. They petitioned the British King, George III, for a suitable vessel to send to the south Pacific. The young King with his interest in things astronomical, instructed the Admiralty to find a suitable ship and promised £4000 towards the project. They chose a small merchant collier the Earl of Pembroke, built in Whitby, Yorkshire. She was the ideal vessel for a long voyage. Her huge hold would be able to carry all the necessary foods, stores and equipment and with a flat bottom she could run onto any suitable sandy beach for repairs. They renamed her Endeavour and in August 1768 she went into Deptford Dockyard on the river Thames for refitting for the voyage to the South Pacific.

Shipwrights and carpenters set to work. Endeavour's hull was double sheathed with wood, and coated with white stuff, a thick mixture of white lead and grease to prevent attack from marine borers. Her upper sides were painted with varnish of pine, and she was finished in the Royal Naval colours of blue, red and yellow.

The weather deck

On the weather deck a new tiller with a kick-up to clear the great cabin stove chimney was added, and another chimney was fixed forward for the firehearth (stove). All the deck equipment was renewed or repaired, and two standard binnacles to hold the compasses were bolted to the deck beside the wheel.

Extra decks and cabins were needed to accommodate the 94 people who were to come aboard. Officers and crew, the Royal Society astronomer and a party of natural scientists were to join the ship.

Lower deck

A new lower deck was added running the full length of the ship. This had to be fitted onto the existing beams, and resulted in an unusually high deck height forward and a very low one, just 4 feet 6 inches (1.2 metres) aft.

A large iron firehearth was fitted forward, with shelves, lockers and a small table for the cook John Thompson and his assistants who prepared all the meals. Cabins and storerooms were built on either side for the carpenter John Satterley and the boatswain John Gathrey, who were responsible for the day to day maintenance and condition of the ship.

Swinging mess tables were fitted along both sides of the ship for the seamen and the marines who ate in groups of six, seated on their sea chests. Above each table small shelves were fixed to hold their bowls and mugs. Here on their mess deck, the seamen ate, socialised and slept slinging their hammocks just 14 inches apart. There was no such thing as privacy for an 18th century seaman.

Aft of the mess deck, cabins were built for the master Robert Molyneux, the 2nd Lieutenant Zachary Hicks, 3rd Lieutenant John Gore, the surgeon William Munkhouse, the gunner Stephen Forwood and the Captain's clerk Richard Orton. Measuring just 6 feet (1.8 metres) by 5 feet (1.5 metres), and with a deck height of only 4 feet 6 inches (1.2 metres) they provided little comfort, but just enough space to sleep and store a few personal items. Each had a tiny external port (window) which could be opened to provide fresh air and light when they were at anchor, and a small internal sash window. The carpenters fitted lockers, but the officers brought their own furniture, bedding, curtains and any equipment such as telescopes and sextants that were necessary to carry out their duties.

The area between these cabins served as a mess for the midshipmen and mates, and they slung their hammocks here at night. It was dark and cramped. Two large loading hatches in the stern were sealed when at sea, however at anchor they could be opened and then this mess area was light and airy.

above: *A four pounder replica carriage gun. Endeavour's guns regularly fire blanks at appropriate, and sometimes inappropriate moments;* **above right:** *Working the capstan to lift heavy gear, while a shipmate plays a lively tune;* **right:** *On her first day sailing off Fremantle, Endeavour shows her style;* **top right:** *2nd Lieutenant Zachary Hicks' tiny cabin has only 4'6" (1.2m) headroom; and The seamen's mess deck;* **top left:** *Original 18th century plans show the position of cabins and storage over the four decks.*

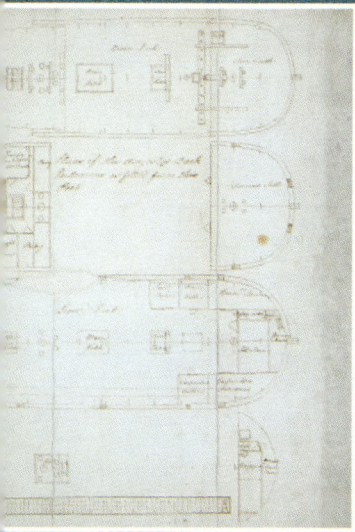

The after deck

Directly above the lower deck was the after deck with the great cabin, and the captain's and gentlemen's cabins. The great cabin was traditionally the captain's, however on Endeavour, Cook shared it with the gentlemen. It was spacious and well lit by four large stern sash windows and two quarter windows. The stern windows were fitted with heavy wooden deadlights (shutters), which could be lowered during stormy weather. Two curved cupboards which had been on the Earl of Pembroke were kept and lockers were added below the windows. The Admiralty provided a stove for heating, a small serving table, a large wooden dining table and chairs.

James Cook requested green baize cloth to carpet the deck; however the Navy Board always conscious of costs and status, gave him the cheaper painted floorcloth, an early type of linoleum.

The area between the cabins was the commissioned officers' mess. Here they ate and worked on their logs and charts under the large deck hatch. Two pantry's were fitted onto this deck; one for storing food and drink was tucked on the port side (left) under the deck, and the starboard(right) pantry was used to store cooking equipment, crockery, cutlery and food. Here their servants prepared their food before taking it to the firehearth for cooking.

All the sleeping cabins were fitted with storage lockers and swinging cots. Most had a small internal sash (window) as well as a tiny external hatch high enough above the waterline to open during good sailing weather. Charles Green the astronomer once found a flying fish in his cot which had

left: James Cook shared the great cabin with the naturalists; furniture and personal items have been carefully replicated; **top:** *The officer's mess has a folding table based on an original owned by James Cook;* **middle left:** *Astronomer Charles Green's cabin, with swinging cot and extract from his journal;* **middle right:** *3rd Lieutenant John Gore's cabin; most of the textiles on board have been hand loomed, hand sewn and made to original 18th century patterns;* **bottom:** *The captain's cabin with his furniture, books, charts and personal items.*

ome in through this hatch. Cook's cabin had a door to the reat cabin as well as one leading into the lobby. This gave im quick access to the quarter deck when needed. Joseph Banks, naturalist, had large storage cupboards fitted into his abin for his equipment and belongings. He and his fellow aturalist Dr Solander often preferred to sleep in the great abin during the voyage.

The hold

n the hold at the bottom of the ship, two small decks were dded; an aft flat provided a cabin for the purser, store oom for the captain, a bread room and dried fish room; he magazine with its gunpowder was traditionally fitted on the forward flat and lined with lead, then plastered to keep the powder dry. A marine would have been on duty here to stop anyone entering without the Captain's permission. Extra lockers, cupboards and shelves were fitted wherever needed.

On the 18th May, His Majesty's Bark Endeavour came out of dry dock ready to be rigged and provisioned. Twelve swivel guns and ten four-pounder guns (cannons) were fitted in place. Gunpowder, ammunition, small arms, cutlasses, casks of food, water, beer, spirits, extra sails and ropes, blocks, paint, varnish, chickens, pigs, sheep, oxen and a milking goat were loaded on board. Thousands of items were needed to support 94 men for three years voyage around the world.

Before she sailed from Plymouth on 25 August 1768, the shipwrights built a wooden platform over the tiller on the quarter deck, to provide a bridge for the gentlemen to use.

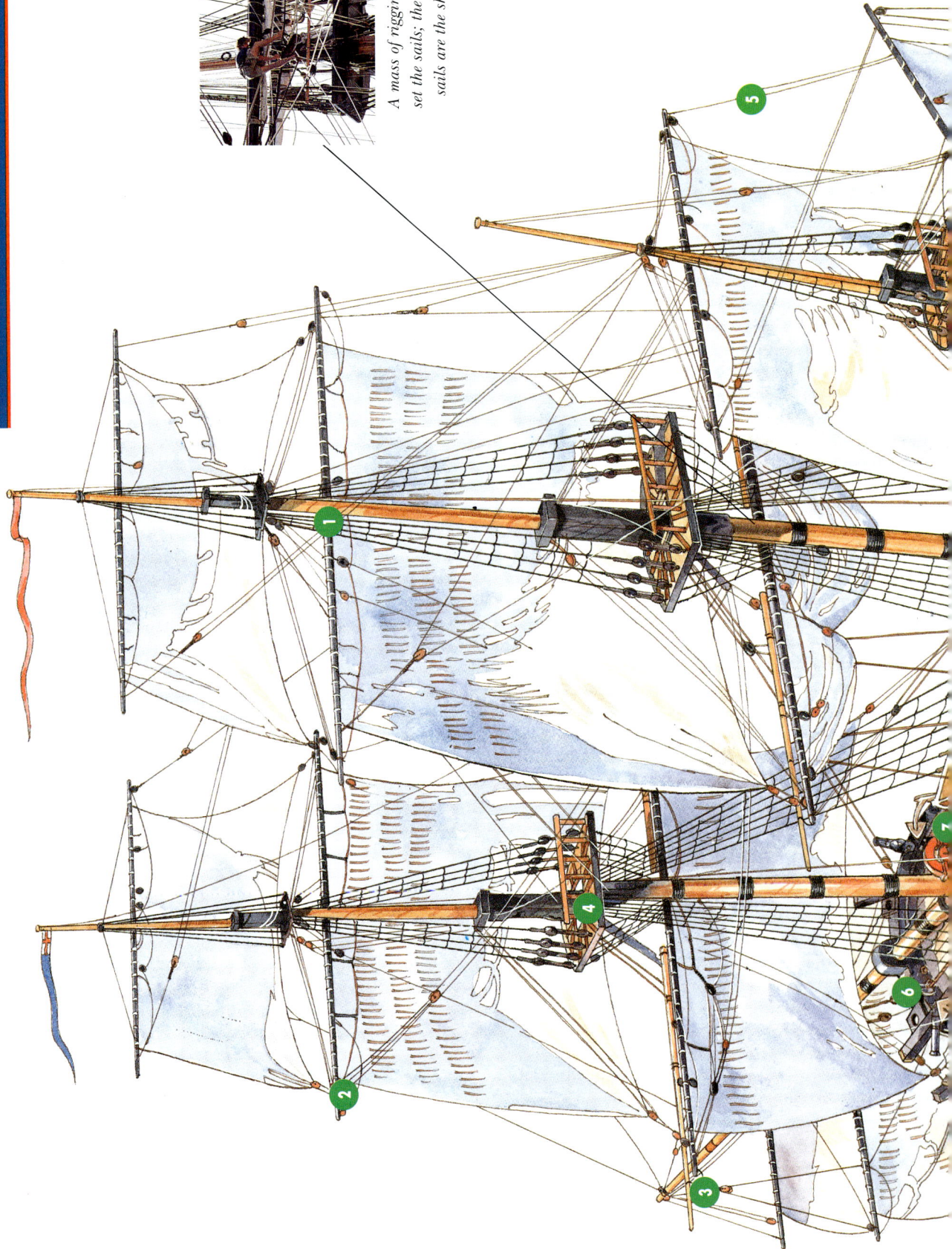

A mass of rigging is needed to set the sails; the wind and the sails are the ship's engines

80 seamen ate and socialised on the mess deck. Like their 18th century fellows, today's crew sling their hammocks and sleep here

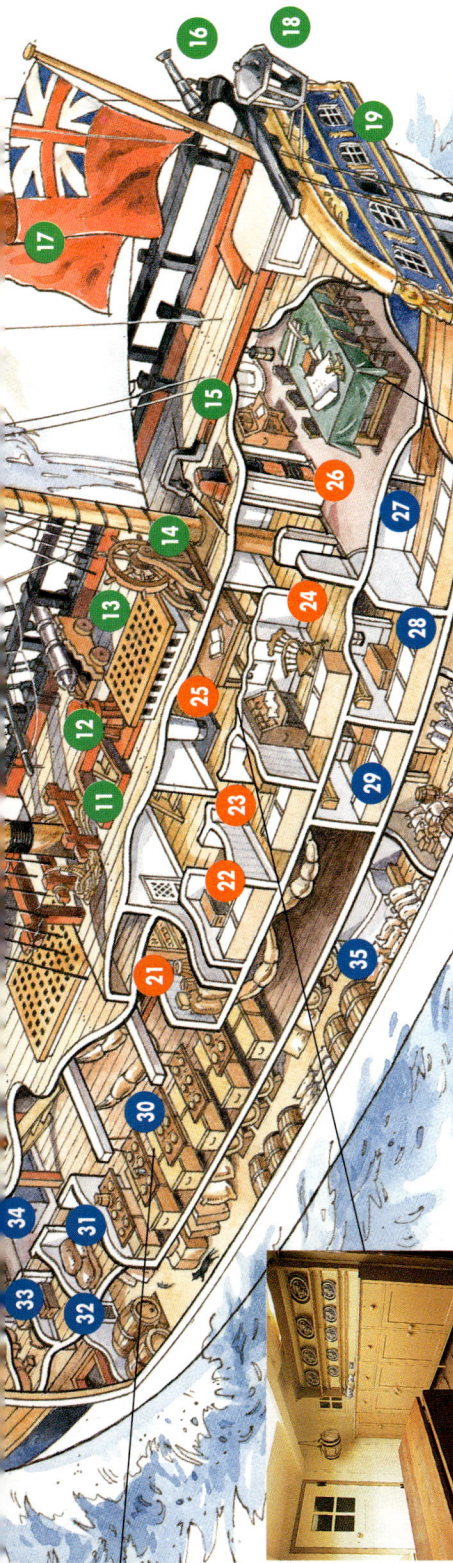

Here the officers stored their personal crockery, glassware, cutlery and linen, nothing was provided by the Navy

Endeavour had four decks; the weather deck on top; below this the after-fall deck running half the length of the ship from the stern; then the lower or mess deck; and finally the hold.

1. Mainmast
2. Yard
3. Bowsprit
4. Tops
5. Blocks
6. Seats of ease - two wooden lavatories for the seamen
7. Ship's bell marks the rhythm of shipboard life
8. Best bower anchor
9. Windlass used to raise and lower the anchors
10. Companion (ladder) to lower deck
11. Companion to after fall deck
12. Capstan, a winch to move heavy gear and the ship in anchorage
13. Carriage gun, fired four pounder shot. Ten on board
14. Wheel connected by ropes to the tiller
15. Tiller with kick-up to clear the cabin stove chimney
16. Swivel gun to repel boats and boarders, 12 on board
17. The 18th century Red Ensign, with the Queen Anne Union flag
18. Stern lantern
19. Stern windows
20. Rudder, connected by chains and ropes to the tiller
21. Pantry stored provisions for the people on the after-fall deck
22. The naturalist's cabin, Dr Daniel Carl Solander
23. The artists' cabin, Sydney Parkinson & Alexander Buchan
24. The captain's cabin, 1st Lieutenant James Cook
25. Officer's mess where they ate, relaxed and worked on their journals

The great cabin with the captain's cabin leading off

26. Great Cabin where the captain and the naturalists ate and worked
27. The 2nd Lieutenant's cabin, Zachary Hicks
28. The surgeon's cabin, William Brougham Munkhouse
29. The gunner's cabin, Stephen Forwood
30. The crew's mess deck with swinging tables and hammocks
31. Sail room
32. The boatswain's cabin, John Gathrey
33. Boatswain's storeroom
34. Firehearth (stove) all the ship's meals were cooked here
35. The hold where all the supplies needed for the journey were stored
36. Longboat, the heaviest of the ship's boats
37. Pinnace, used for scouting forays

JAMES COOK, HIS OFFICERS & SEAMEN

James Cook was born in the village of Marton, Yorkshire on 27 October 1728, the second son of a Scottish farm labourer. From the age of 18 he was apprenticed to John Walker, a shipowner at Whitby, and spent the next ten years sailing small merchant colliers along the eastern coast of Britain and across the North Sea to the Baltic. At the age of 28 Cook turned down the offer of his own ship, and joined the Royal Navy. It is not certain why he did this. However time proved he was an ambitious man, and with England on a war footing with France, promotion and prize money may have provided the incentive. Cook signed on board *HMS Eagle*, at Wapping, London on 17 June 1755, with the rank of ableseaman.

As an experienced seaman he gained quick promotion, and two years later passed his master's examination. Appointed to the new 64 gun ship of the line *HMS Pembroke*, Cook left for Canada as part of Admiral Boscawen's squadron sent to fight the French. After Quebec fell, Cook stayed in Newfoundland, charting and surveying the coastline. He produced charts that were accurate enough to be used for the next 100 years.

In December 1762, he returned to England and married Elizabeth Batts, 13 years his junior. Just four months later Cook was promoted to surveyor and returned to Canada aboard *HMS Antelope*. His life followed this pattern, summers surveying in Canada and winters at home with Elizabeth and his children until 15 April 1768, when the Admiralty appointed him to the rank of 1st Lieutenant and gave him command of *His Majesty's Bark*

Endeavour. Cook was 40 years of age, an experienced and competent seaman, a proven navigator and surveyor, however he had never had command of a vessel nor experience of a long sea voyage. It was on board Endeavour that Cook "cut his teeth" as a world explorer.

Endeavour's crew were young, most under 30 years of age. Little is known about them apart from their ages, place of birth and rank. Some of them smoked or chewed tobacco which they purchased from the purser, and some bought bedding and clothes when they arrived. They were all experienced sailors, mainly from Britain and they willingly signed on for the voyage.

Cook's fellow officers were reliable, experienced seamen. Second in command was Lieutenant Zachary Hicks, from Stepney in London. He was 29 years of age and had already been 15 years at sea. Third Lieutenant John Gore, in his mid thirties, had been twice around the world aboard *HMS Dolphin* and had visited the newly discovered island of Tahiti. His knowledge of the south seas was to be valuable to the captain. Gore regularly shot birds and animals for Endeavour's stores, played in an archery contest with a Tahitian chief, caught the first stingray in Botany Bay and killed the first kangaroo in Australia.

Two others joined from Dolphin. Robert Molyneux, just 22 years old, signed on as master and Richard Pickersgill, 19, as his mate. Their duties included navigation, the correct stowage of ballast and stores, and responsibility for safe anchorage. Pickersgill was a good surveyor and drew a number of charts during the voyage. Second masters' mate was Charles Clerke, 25 from Essex. An excellent officer he kept his shipmates amused with stories about giants, having already written a book on the subject. He was devoted to Cook, and continued to serve with him on the second and third voyages of discovery.

Endeavour had three midshipmen - John Bootie, Jonathan Munkhouse, younger brother to the surgeon and Patrick Saunders. Saunders jumped ship in Batavia after he was suspected of a drunken assault on the Captain's clerk Richard Orton, during which Orton had part of his ears cut off.

Orton was a careless worker and in Cook's opinion *"a man not without faults"*. Isaac Smith, cousin to Cook's wife, was promoted to midshipman during the voyage and assisted Cook in surveying and chart making. Cook gave him the honour of being the first Englishman to step onto Australian soil.

To keep the peace and protect the landing parties ashore, Endeavour received twelve marines under the command of Sergeant John Edgcumbe who Cook called *"a good soldier, very much a gentleman, and well deserving of promotion"*. Cook kept his word and Edgcumbe served as lieutenant in Resolution during the second voyage.

Little is remembered about the ordinary seamen who sailed on Endeavour. However Cook who knew them best wrote: *"They have gone through the fatigues and dangers of the whole Voyage with that cheerfulness and Allertness that will always do Honour to British Seamen."*

left: *Portrait of Captain James Cook by Nathanial Dance painted after his return from the second voyage;* top left: *A young officer shaving;* top middle: *A midshipman;* top right: *3rd Lieutenant John Gore;* bottom: *An 18th century ship's carpenter with the tools of his trade.*

The Royal Society, Charles Green & The Transit of Venus

Since 1660, The Royal Society of London had dedicated itself to the advancement of practical knowledge and by the 18th century, their journal "Philosophical Transactions" had become a melting-pot for international scientific ideas. In 1761, although Europe was in the middle of the Seven Years War, the Royal Society took part in the Paris Academy's observations of the transit of Venus across the sun. By calculating the time it took the planet Venus to travel across the sun, it was hoped to be able to find through various mathematical calculations, the distance of the sun from earth. This measurement would be the first step to measuring the universe. Unfortunately the results were disappointing, and the Royal Society, not to be outdone by the French, decided to co-ordinate the next international effort in 1769. On this occasion 151 observers would watch the transit of Venus from 77 different countries around the world. The Royal Society proposed to send a ship to a suitable island in the South Pacific where it was hoped that good weather would be guaranteed.

Charles Green the astronomer, was 35 years old when he walked on board Endeavour with his servant John Reynolds. Born in Yorkshire, the son of a local farmer, Green had been assistant to the Astronomer Royal Charles Maskelyne. A cheerful and engaging man, Green was fond of a prank and always happy to share his knowledge. Early in the voyage he taught Cook and his officers to use the lunar distance method to find longitude, and they discussed their findings when they sat down to dinner in the great cabin. Cook often relied on Green's daily latitude and longitude figures, especially during the difficult time sailing along the east coast of Australia.

As chief observer for the Transit of Venus, Green was responsible for organising the viewing, and for collecting and working out the figures which would be handed to the Royal Society at the end of the voyage. When the ship reached Tahiti in April 1769, Green lived ashore in a special fort built to house and protect the shore party and observation tent. Cook gave a clear description of the tent and the latest up-to-date astronomical equipment in his journal:

"The astronomical clock, made by Shelton and furnished with a gridiron pendulum, was set up in the middle of one end of a large tent, in a frame of wood made for the purpose at Greenwich, fixed firm and as low in the ground as the door of the clock-case would admit…The pendulum was adjusted to exactly the same length as it had been at Greenwich. Without the end of the tent facing the clock, and 12 feet from it, stood the observatory, in which were set up the journeyman clock and astronomical quadrant; this last, made by Mr Bird of one foot radius, stood upon the head of a large cask fixed firm in the ground, and well filled with wet heavy sand… The telescopes made use of in the observations were - two reflecting ones of two feet focus each, made by the late Mr James Short, one of which was furnished with an object glass micrometer."

Cook named the promontory on which the fort was built - Fort Venus.

The morning of Saturday 3 June was bright and clear, and three parties prepared for the event. Charles Green with Cook and Dr Solander were to observe from Fort Venus while Lieutenant Hicks, Master's Mates Charles Clerke and Richard Pickersgill, with Midshipman Patrick Saunders, took the ship's pinnace to a small island in the east. The previous day Lieutenant John Gore, Surgeon William Munkhouse and secretary Herman Sporing, had rowed the long boat to an island 10 miles to the west, and Banks went along to spend the time collecting plants.

It was a tense time for the observers who needed to carefully note the time it took the planet to pass over the surface of the sun. The sighting was successfully completed and everyone gathered back at Fort Venus to celebrated with a good meal and drink. Unfortunately the final world wide results were again disappointing, with widely

arying figures. The problem of timing eclipses would not be
olved until the invention of a more accurate telescope.

On the voyage home Green and his young servant John
Reynolds died of dysentery in January 1771. When his notes
were handed to the Royal Society, they were found to be
disordered and incomplete; perhaps he had expected to use
he run home from Batavia to work
n them. The Astronomer Royal
Maskelyne publicly criticised him,
however Cook defended Green, aware
nd grateful for his important contribution
o the Endeavour's navigation.

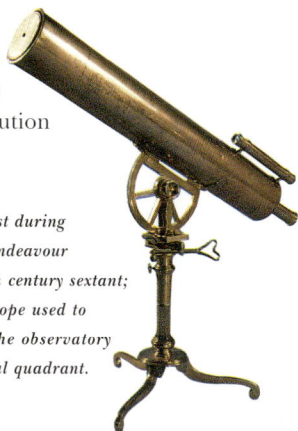

*op: Matavai Bay Tahiti by William Hodges artist during
ook's second voyage, little had changed since Endeavour
nchored here four years earlier;* **bottom left:** *18th century sextant;*
ottom middle: *Mr James Short's reflecting telescope used to
bserve the Transit;* **bottom right:** *A mock-up of the observatory
nt showing Shelton's clock and the astronomical quadrant.*

JOSEPH BANKS & HIS GROUP

Joseph Banks at 24, was already a respected botanist and member of the Royal Society. A wealthy young man he had inherited estates at Revesby Abbey in Lincolnshire, and after studying at Eton and Oxford, set off on his first foreign botany voyage to Newfoundland and Labrador on the 32 gun naval frigate *Niger*. Returning in 1767 he heard of the proposed voyage to the South Seas. He applied to take a group of natural scientists and artists on the voyage at his own expense. He was accepted and to his great delight his friend and teacher, Dr Daniel Carl Solander agreed to accompany him.

Daniel Solander was 34 years of age, and had studied botany in Sweden under the famous Swedish botanist Linnaeus. He had met Banks at the newly established British Museum in London where he had joined the staff to classify their collection. During the voyage he worked identifying and classifying the plants and animals they found. Solander's personal clerk Herman Diedrich Sporing, a fellow Swede, came on board as secretary.

Sporing had also studied medicine and watch making and during the voyage Cook often asked him to mend the ship's instruments. He was also able to repair the astronomical quadrant after it had been stolen by some of the natives on Tahiti.

The plants and specimens would also need to be drawn and painted while still fresh and brightly coloured. Banks engaged two artists, Sydney Parkinson and Alexander Buchan. Parkinson, a 23 year old Scot, had been working for Banks in London drawing his Newfoundland collection, and jumped at the chance. During the voyage he worked tirelessly, often sitting up all night drawing and writing in his journal. He finished 955 drawings of floral and 377 of fauna, before he died of dysentery on the voyage home. The other artist Alexander Buchan was employed to draw landscapes and figures. Little is known about his life before he joined Endeavour, and he completed few drawings as he died of an epileptic fit shortly after the ship reached Tahiti. His drawing of Endeavour's watering place in the Bay of Good Success, is one of the earliest visual records of a meeting between the natives and Europeans.

top left to right: *The great cabin where the naturalists often worked on their specimens late into the night; the artist Sydney Parkinson; Dr Daniel Carl Solander, Swedish naturalist; Joseph Banks naturalist, funded the botanical side of the Endeavour voyage; watercolours* **by** *Parkinson* **top:** *Bomarea edulis collected on the island of Raza, Brazil, edible root;* **left:** *Solanum viride collected in Tahiti, the leaves were eaten baked;* **right:** *Arripis trutta growing to a length of one metre it was enjoyed by everyone on board, New Zealand and Australia.*

Banks took four servants, all of whom had been trained to collect specimens. His good servant and friend of ten years James Roberts, who had looked after him at Oxford and accompanied him on board the *Niger* on the Newfoundland trip, gave a glimpse of their working relationship in his journal: we *"drew lots for places in the small tent when camping…here was no master and Slave but a willingness to assist each other put us all upon an equality except in point of Learning and Philosophical knowledge"*. Young Peter Bricoe and two black servants George Dorlton and Thomas Richmond came down from Revesby Abbey.

The natural scientists worked in the Great Cabin from early morning until late at night, stopping only for meals or very rough weather. They dissected, preserved, identified and drew the plants, fish, insects, animals and shells they found. While sailing they fished by line and net to catch sea creatures, and when there was no wind Banks took his skiff and rowed around the ship collecting specimens to examine and to eat. Everyone on board was interested in the scientists work, for it was a distraction from the sometimes boring routine of life at sea. As Dr Solander wrote from Rio, the sailors helped them with their work and *"…soon became such good philosophers that they even recollected the different names and could remember what we had shown them, and consequently could look out for new ones."*

Never before had there been a natural history voyage on such a scale. Banks took a vast amount of equipment, a comprehensive library of over 150 books, special equipment for dissecting and preserving, microscopes, a new sea telescope, paper for drying plants, tin trunks for storage, wooden cases, boxes and hundred of other items including beads and mirrors for trading.

As well as their botanical work, Banks and his group compiled the first social study of the South Sea natives. They recorded buildings, clothes, agriculture, arts, weapons and musical instruments even attempting to write down their songs. They studied the various languages and compiled the first dictionaries of the islands. Banks and Solander often took on the job of bargaining with the natives, and their knowledge of vegetation and suitable plants and fruits to eat, added to the ship's food stores.

On their return to England, Banks and Solander were enthusiastically welcomed by Society. They were invited to meet the King, who wanted to see their collections of the Pacific; this comprised over 1500 drawings and paintings, over 1000 new plants, more than 500 fish and some 500 birds, together with innumerable invertebrates and a large number of "curiosities"- weapons, musical instruments, music, cloths and jewellery.

Of the nine people who joined Banks' group in 1768 only four survived the voyage - Joseph Banks, his colleague Dr Solander, and his servants Briscoe and Roberts.

THE VOYAGE

South America and the South Seas

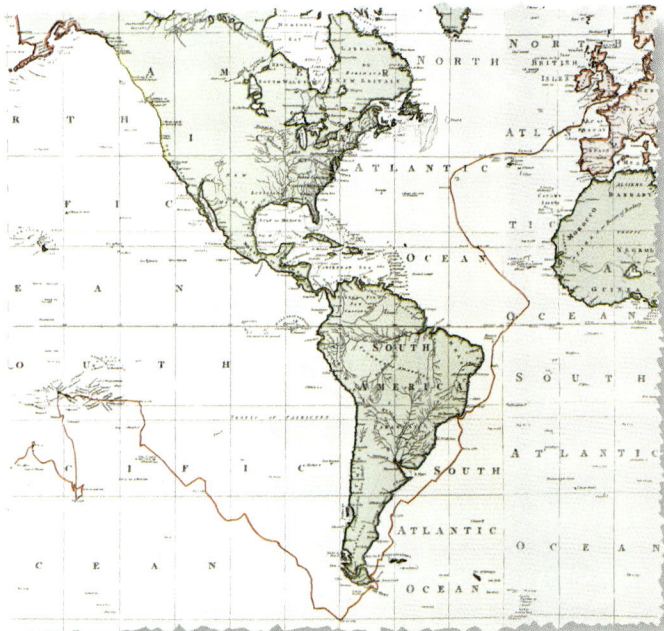

After setting sail from Plymouth on 8 August 1768 Endeavour ran down the coast of Portugal and Spain arriving at the island of Madeira five weeks later. Here Cook took on fresh produce and 3000 gallons of wine, before continuing down the coast of West Africa and across the North Atlantic to South America. On the 13th November, Endeavour arrived in Rio de Janeiro where the Viceroy, believing them to be spies, refused to let anyone ashore without an armed escort. While the artists sketched the bay from the ship's deck, Banks and Solander managed to steal ashore some evenings to gather plants. But the stale-mate continued and tempers flared on shore and on board. Everyone was delighted when they up anchored and sailed out of Rio, dropping down the coast of South America to Cape Horn. All the crew were issued with warm woollen jackets and trousers. It was now December and the Horn was notorious for treacherous weather and quick storms.

Endeavour stopped at Tierra del Fuego to collect fresh water and wood for cooking. This provided the natural scientists with their first chance to meet the natives. An Indian settlement was discovered two miles away, and Banks, Buchan and Parkinson with a group of sailors and marines, walked along the two mile muddy track to investigate and barter for goods. Here Buchan painted the earliest known drawing of the Fuegans. The next day during a botany expedition into the country, a sudden snow storm caught them by surprise. The group was already separated and were forced to sleep overnight in the open, with no protection. Sadly Thomas Richmond and George Dolton died of hypothermia. Buchan had suffered an epileptic fit, while Dr Solander and one of the seamen were still very ill by the time they returned to the ship.

Rounding the Cape, Endeavour headed north west into the South Seas. On 13 April 1769 Cook located the new island of King George's Island, now called Tahiti, and anchored

in Matavai Bay. The Tahitians welcomed them and gave permission to build a fort for viewing the Transit of Venus.

Soon after work on the fort had started there was a clash of cultures. The idea of private ownership was alien to the Tahitians and a native snatched a musket from one of the guards. An officer fired after him, killing him and wounding others. Cook ordered the crew not to punish theft in this way and avoided further bloodshed.

Pilfering continued to be a problem - clothes, iron nails, Dr Munkhouse's snuff box, even the astronomical quadrant went missing. Endeavour stayed in Tahiti for three months. Everyone on board shared in Tahitian life ashore, and in return many natives visited the ship. The chiefs ate in the great cabin with the captain and his officers. Most of those on board Endeavour

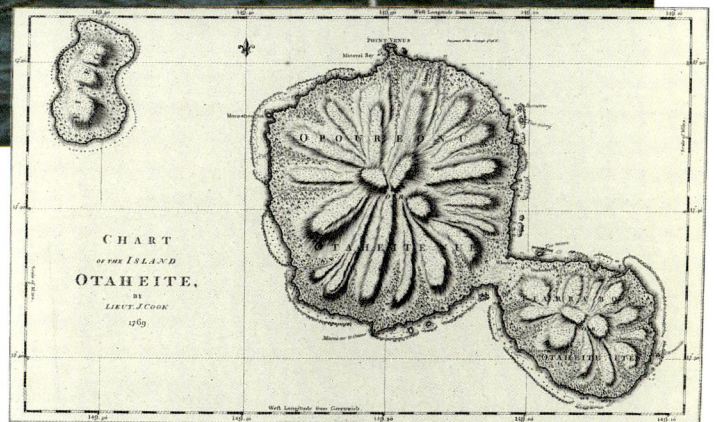

ngaged in sexual liaisons with the women, learned to speak
ome of their language, slept in their houses, ate their foods
nd joined in rituals and entertainments.

Banks and his group kept busy sketching, painting and
ecording Tahitian life, as well as the natural flora and fauna.
Cook and Isaac Smith took the ship's cutter and sailed around
Tahiti, charting and surveying the island. Everyone enjoyed
hemselves and three months of mostly peaceful contact, taught
he Europeans respect for Tahitian society.

After dismantling Fort Venus, Endeavour was ready to leave,
nd it was a sad farewell on both sides. A young chief Tupaia
nd his servant sailed with them, and piloted the ship to the
Polynesian islands of Huahine, Raiatea, Tahoa and Rurutu.
Cook surveyed and charted them, noting their positions for
he first time as the Society Islands.

With the first part of his orders completed Cook now put
nto action his "Secret Orders" to look for the Great South Land
which was thought to lie in the great expanse of uncharted water
to the west. For several weeks Endeavour sailed across the Pacific
with many false sightings of land, until 6 October 1769, when
Nicholas Young, sitting at the mast head shouted "Land"; they
had reached the east coast of New Zealand.

*top: A 20th century 'young Nick' sights New Zealand from the foremast of
Endeavour; left: Alexander Buchan's drawing of natives and their hut at Tierra
del Fuego; right: James Cook and Isaac Smith sailed around Tahiti (Otaheti) and
charted the island in 1769.*

THE VOYAGE

New Zealand

regularity to the parts of a Song which they chanted in a very martial tone...(one of the men)...in bending forward, throwing his Arms behind him, elevating his head, staring wildly upwards, and thrusting his tongue forward...at the close of the song, pronouncing the last sentence with a strong hoarse expirations - the rest followed his example in the last manoeuvre. We commended the performance and they obliged us with a repetition of it."

The Europeans' inability to understand Maori ritual challenges often led to bloodshed. However as Endeavour sailed from bay to bay, some tribes welcomed them and traded fish and vegetables for cloth, beads and nails. Natives came aboard where they were shown around the ship, ate and drank and in return entertained the crew with songs. At Uawa, (Tolaga Bay) Endeavour spent six days, mixing with the people and collecting wood, water and plants. The Tahitian and Maori languages were similar, and Tupaia who spoke several Polynesian languages acted as interpreter. He became such a favourite of the Uawa people that for many years children were named after him.

During their six months circumnavigating the two islands Cook and Banks learned a great deal about Maori life. They noted regional and tribal differences, dialect, agriculture, settlement patterns, weapons, canoes and art. A Maori boy on a visit to Endeavour said of Cook: "...he came up on deck again and came to where I and my two boy-companions were, and patted our heads with his hand...My companions said. This is the leader of the ship, which is proved by his kindness to us; and also he is so very fond of children." Cook in turn came to admire the Maori's courage, virtue and beauty.

On Saturday 31 March 1770, Endeavour sailed past Cape Farewell and left New Zealand heading towards New Holland (Australia).

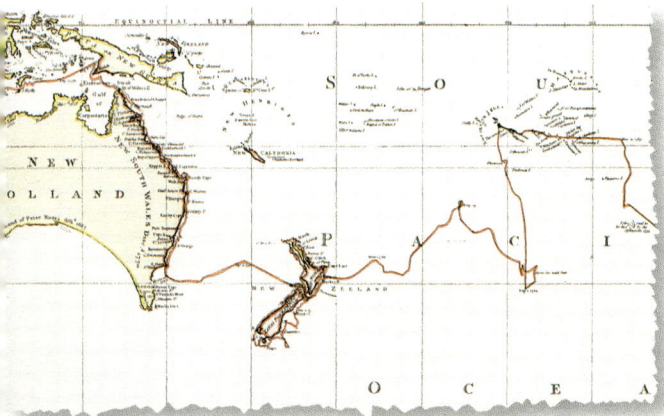

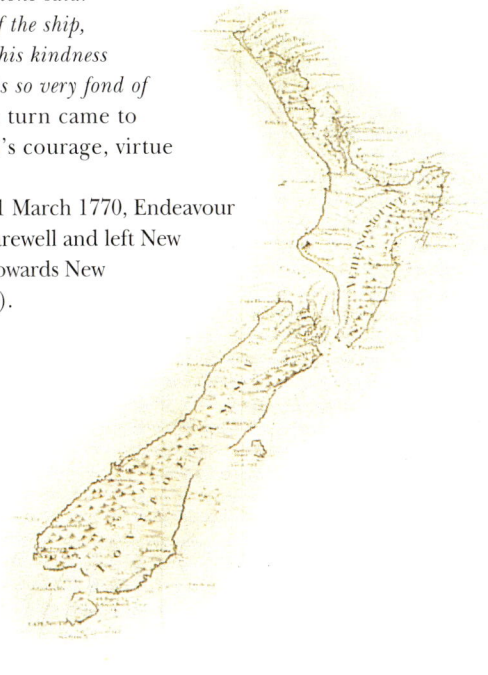

Nick Young received the captain's promised reward of rum for first sighting the white cliff peninsular called by the natives Te Kuri-a-Pao, and named by Cook, Young Nick's Head. Cook proceeded with caution; Abel Tasman who first visited this land in the 17th century had reported hostile natives, who had killed several of his men. In need of fresh water and hoping to barter for food, Cook anchored in a deep natural harbour. A series of meetings and misunderstandings led to the shooting of several Maoris and sickened by the violence, Cook sailed on, naming the place Poverty Bay.

Endeavour spent the next six months circumnavigating New Zealand, charting and surveying, proving that this land was in fact two separate islands.

Time after time Endeavour was attacked by natives, spears were thrown, war dances and speeches made, all usually in the form of ritual challenges. Surgeon Munkhouse described one such event when seven canoes with 160 warriors gathered under Endeavour's stern:

"They treated us with a kind of Heiva or war dance performed by striking their paddles upon the gunwall...beating time in exact

far left: *Endeavour visits Doubtful Bay New Zealand, March 1996;* insets: *Endeavour anchors in Pickersgill Harbour in the same spot as depicted by John Webber the artist aboard Discovery on the second voyage. Note the tents on shore and the washing out to dry;* left: *Dressed in traditional costumes a Maori war canoe approaches Endeavour's stern;* above: *Cook's 1770 chart of New Zealand clearly shows his skill as a surveyor.*

The Voyage

East coast of New Holland (Australia)

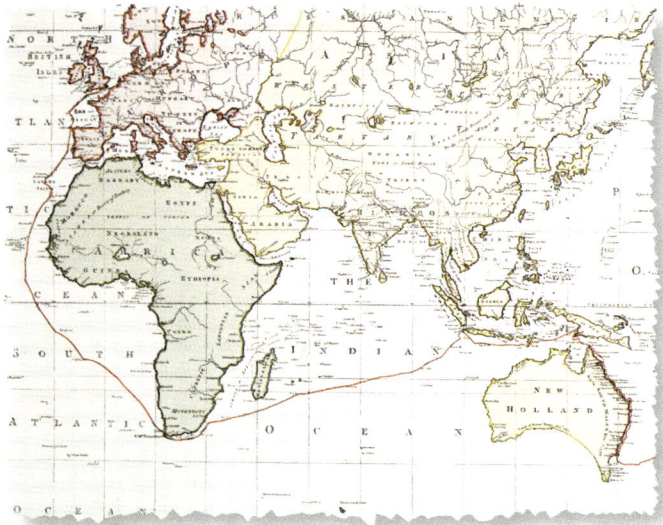

On 19th April 1770, Lieutenant Zachary Hicks standing watch on deck saw land at 6am. Cook named this Point Hicks (now known as Cape Everard), and Endeavour had reached the east coast of New Holland (Australia).

Eight days later Cook, Banks, Solander and Tupaia put off in the yawl but the surf made a landing impossible. The following day Cook took Endeavour into a sheltered bay where his young cousin-in-law Isaac Smith was given the honour of being the first to step ashore. Cook recorded that the few Aboriginals they saw were shy, lean, naked and generally ignored the Europeans. They refused the trading gifts offered and "all they seem'd to want was for us to be gone" he wrote. Here they found good supplies of fish and oysters, and Endeavour's sportsman Lieutenant Gore, killed the first stingray, which made good eating on board. The botanists gathered such large quantities of new plants that Cook named this place Botany Bay.

Aboriginal fires followed them day and night as they sailed up the coast. Whether these were natural burning or messages of the ship's progress they did not know.

For the next four months Cook sailed north charting more than 2000 miles of the unknown eastern coast of Australia. He named headlands, bays and mountains as he went - Cape Howe, the Pigeon House, Point Danger, Moreton Bay, Sandy Cape, Bustard Bay (which gave them such good birds to eat), Great Keppel Island, Thirsty Sound (where they could not find fresh water), Halifax Bay (where Banks found cabbage palms). They passed Cape Tribulation where, as Cook wrote *"began all our troubles"*.

Endeavour had become trapped by the Great Barrier Reef.

Unknown to Cook the vast reef ran at an angle to the coast forming a great funnel. This funnel was widest at the south and gradually narrowed until the ship ran onto a coral reef at high tide. It was a few minutes before 11 pm, 11 June 1770. Cook was immediately on deck and ordered everything heavy thrown overboard to lighten the ship. During

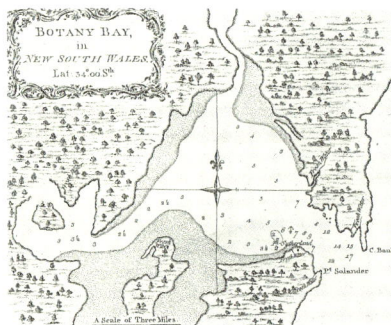

the next twenty three hours every man, including Banks and his group, took their turn at the pumps to keep the water level from gaining. As the tide rose Endeavour was successfully hauled off the reef. Endeavour's crew had proved their worth. Banks was later to comment on the officer's calmness and the seamen's *"absence of oaths"*, during this dangerous time.

A landing spot had to be found quickly, but it was not until four days later that they located a sandy beach at the head of a river. Cook ran the ship's flat bottom safely onto the beach on 16 June 1770, and named this Endeavour River. During the next seven weeks, the carpenter John Satterley and his mates repaired the damage while the seamen cleaned, scraped and painted the ship. Banks and his group explored the country, gathering large quantities of unknown plants and animals. Surgeon Munkhouse rowed up the river to collect scurvy grass and food for the sick. Here they saw and shot their first kangaroo, the strange animal that would amaze people in Europe. They made friendly contact with local Aboriginals, noting their language, weapons,

Cook took the ship back within the reef. For the next week with the ships boats in front sounding the depth, they sailed slowly by day and anchored by night. This way Cook took Endeavour through the sea he was to call *The Labyrinth*, until they reached Cape York.

Just before sunset on 21 August Cook landed and climbed a nearby hill. Here he hoisted the English colours and took possession of the whole of the east coast of Australia in the name of King George III. Heading through the strait which he now knew separated Australia from New Guinea, Endeavour sailed for the Dutch East Indies colony of Batavia, to repair the ship before continuing homewards.

above: Endeavour rides above the Great Barrier Reef in Queensland where she grounded in 1770;
inset: An engraving of the original ship beached for repairs with the tents set up ashore at Endeavour River;
far left: Cook's chart of Botany Bay; left: The naturalists discovered flannel flowers like these at Botany Bay;
right: Parkinson's painting of a uniquely Australian plant Banksia ericifolia, named in honour of Joseph Banks in 1781.

t, canoes, food and hunting skills. Cook was to write of the east ast natives: *"..they may appear to some to be the most wretched people bon Earth, but in reality they are far more happier than we Europeans".*

Once repairs were finished Cook attempted to gain access rough the reef to the open sea. Suddenly the winds dropped d Endeavour was swept back towards certain shipwreck. Just in me, a breeze came up and a channel in the reef appeared.

HEALTH & DIET AT SEA

After two years at sea Cook arrived in Batavia having lost just eight of the 94 people who set sail from England. Alexander Weir the quartermaster and ableseaman Peter Flower had accidentally drowned; Forby Sutherland ableseaman, died of consumption and was buried at Botany Bay; John Reading the boatswain's mate died from drinking too much rum; Marine Private William Greenslade committed suicide by jumping overboard. Joseph Banks had lost three of his group - the artist Alexander Buchan from epilepsy, and servants Thomas Richmond and George Dorlton of hypothermia during the freak snow storm at Tierra del Fuego.

This was a remarkable record. Ships on long sea voyages often lost half of their crew to scurvy. Scurvy was caused by a lack Vitamin C, and although this was not known it was understood that a diet of fresh foods prevented the disease. The symptoms of scurvy were depression and fatigue, followed by haemorrhaging, swollen joints and eventually a painful death. Although there were mild cases of scurvy on board Endeavour, all recovered after the surgeon administered lemon and orange essence.

In an attempt to prevent scurvy the Admiralty had issued Endeavour extra foods thought to be useful and ordered Surgeon William Brougham Munkhouse to keep a record of their effect. Sauerkraut (pickled cabbage),

ried beef stock and malt were added to the daily diet. Fresh
oods were supplied whenever possible, however the problem
as how to keep food fresh before the invention of modern
anning and refrigeration.

By 18th century standards the seamen's diet was good if
omewhat boring. They received meat four times a week, and a
ound of biscuits and a gallon of beer daily. On the three days
eat was not served, fish or cheese was substituted. Vegetables
ere added whenever available. Breakfast on Endeavour was a
orm of porridge made of wheat, with additional beef stock
dded. This was so good that even Banks and his group ate it
very morning.

Luckily for Endeavour she was not often away from land for
ny great length of time. This meant that fresh greens, meats
nd water were frequently available. Cook sent parties of seamen
shore to collect "greens" and Banks' and Solander's knowledge
f plants helped to identify the most effective vegetable sources.
ook encouraged everyone on board to eat a varied diet
henever possible as he wrote in his journal: *"Many of my people,
fficers as well as seamen, at first disliked celery, scurvy grass etc, being
oiled in the peas and wheat: and some refused to eat it: but as this had
o effect on my conduct, this obstinate kind of prejudice, by little and
ttle wore off; they began to like it as well as the others."*

Banks and the officers shot birds and animals for the pot,
nd the Pacific Ocean was a rich source of food, providing a
reat variety of fish, oysters and turtles. Although they did at
mes have shortages of fresh foods, it was never for very long

Unfortunately Surgeon William Munkhouse did not leave
medical journal, but the ship's logs record a small number
f men ill, most from stomach disorders and fevers. The usual
omplaints at sea were salt water ulcers, and ruptures from the
eavy manual work.

By fairly dividing all foods, encouraging everyone to eat widely
f a variety of fresh vegetables and fruits, short sea voyages and his
nsistence on a clean ship and crew, Cook kept Endeavour's crew
t and healthy; until they arrived at the port of Batavia in the
utch East Indies on 11 October 1770. Shortly after arriving Banks
oted how ill the seamen aboard other ships looked: *"our people
owever who truly might be called rosy and plump, for we had not a
ck man among us, jeered and flaunted much at their brother seamens
hite faces".*

Their laughter was short lived. Malaria was endemic at Batavia
nd most of the crew were struck down including the captain.
he exception was the sailmaker John Ravenhill aged 70 and
runk most of the time. The first to die was the surgeon William
unkhouse, followed by Tupaia and his servant Tuahea. Repairing
e damage done by the Great Barrier Reef took weeks, and it
as late December before Cook signed on 19 extra seamen and
t sail for the Cape of Good Hope. Once at sea the bloody flux
dysentry) struck and it spread quickly among the crew already
eakened by malaria. 23 men died on the 11 week voyage to the
ape, including Charles Green the astronomer and his servant,
anks' secretary Herman Sporing and the artist Sydney
arkinson. Cook lost nineteen crew including midshipman
onathan Munkhouse, John Satterley the carpenter and two of
is mates, the one handed cook John Thompson and two
arines. It was a sad and depleted ship that sailed into the Cape
n 14 March 1771.

Master Richard Molyneux, Lieutenant Zachary Hicks and
r Solander were still ill and were sent ashore to recuperate.
owever Lieutenant Gore had regained his health and set off to
imb Table Mountain, while Banks collected more specimens and
sited the town. Endeavour was repaired and cleaned, and with
ew stores and 10 extra crew sailed for St Helena island. Three days

later Robert Molyneux died, and after a short stay on St Helena,
Cook sailed for England in convoy with a large group of merchant
ships. A few days later Lieutenant Zachary Hicks died of
consumption and was buried with due ceremony at sea.

Again it was Nick Young who first sighted land. It was 11 July
1771 and HM Bark Endeavour was home.

Cook reported the state of Endeavour to the Admiralty -
Borne 82, Sick 19, Provisions 21 days of bread, 28 days arrack,
4 days beef, 4 days port, 4 weeks pease, oatmeal or rice, 4 weeks
sugar; water 10 tons. Condition of the Bark: Foul.

top left: *Saturday Night at Sea by Cruikshank a typical scene of sailors relaxing
on the mess deck;* **bottom left:** *An 18th century naval medicine chest;*
top: *Endeavour's surgeon William Brougham Munkhouse who was the first to
die of malaria in Batavia. His younger brother Jonathan, a midshipman on
board, died shortly after;* **bottom:** *18th century painting of ships returning
home to the Thames.*

COOK'S SECOND & THIRD VOYAGES

The Endeavour voyage had been a great success. The Transit of Venus had been successfully observed and Cook had sailed thousands of miles of previously unknown waters. He had charted Tahiti and a large number of new islands, circumnavigated New Zealand, and surveyed the east coast of Australia before proving that a strait lay between it's northern cape and New Guinea. Although he had not found the legendary Great South Land in these waters, there was still the possibility of it lying closer to the Antarctic. The Admiralty were eager to continue and over the next eight years, Cook commanded two further voyages into the Pacific.

During this period he sailed from the Antarctic to the Arctic, crossing the equator many times while sweeping vast areas of unknown water. He proved that the Great South Land did not exist outside the Antarctic Circle and that there was no sea route between the Pacific and the Atlantic in the Arctic Circle.

Using the latest scientific and navigational equipment, he was the first to calculate longitude at sea with great accuracy; he discovered and charted dozens of new islands including the Hervey Islands, Friendly Islands (now Tonga) South Georgia and the Sandwich Islands (now Hawaiian Islands).

Cook's ships were clean and his crews well cared for; he never lost a man to the seaman's disease of scurvy. His humanity was not only reserved for his men for he insisted on good conduct towards the people they visited, and punished by the lash any seaman who transgressed. Aware that his voyages would open the Pacific to European settlement, he worried that this would not benefit the indigenous people.

Paradoxically he was to die by their hands. On 14 February 1779, Cook, with four of his marines, was clubbed to death on Kealakekua Beach in Hawaii.

In his lifetime James Cook won the respect of those who sailed with him, and the acclaim of 18th century society. Today, he is justly recognised as one of the greatest explorers and navigators the world has ever known.

above: *Endeavour sets sail from Table Bay, South Africa on her maiden voyage to Britain 13 January 1997;* right: *John Webber the artist on the third voyage vividly captures the moment of Cook's death on Kealakekua Beach, Hawaii on 14 February 1779.*

IN ASSOCIATION WITH THE NATIONAL MARITIME MUSEUM, GREENWICH, LONDON

Published for HM Bark Endeavour Foundation, Fremantle, Australia, by Addax Retail Publishing Ltd, Hadlow, Kent, U.K. Tel: +44 (0)1732 852030. © Copyright 1997 Addax Retail Publishing Ltd. Great Britain. All rights reserved.
No part of this publication may be reproduced, stored in a retrieval system, or transmitted in any form or by any means, electronic, mechanical, photocopying, recording or otherwise, without prior written permission of the copyright owner.

Text: Antonia Macarthur & John Longley. Photographs and illustrations: Cover photo Richard Poulden: pp1-5 photos John Lancaster: p6 photo Alan Brooke: p7 photos John Lancaster: p 9 photos Alan Brooke, inset photo John Lancaster: p10-11 from left top clockwise, deck plans National Maritime Museum (NMM), John Lancaster, Australian Navy Photographic Unit (ANPU), Richard Garvey, John Lancaster, John Longley: p12 Antonia Macarthur: p13 top & middle left Richard Garvey, middle right ANPU, bottom Antonia Macarthur: p14-15 cutaway David Hobbs after Australian Geographic Society:

p16-17 portrait John Gore by permission Australian National Library, others by permission NMM: p18-19 NMM: p20-21 from left photo by kind permission of Cary Wolinsky (National Geographic Society), Parkinson portrait and his drawings by permission Natural History Museum, Dr Daniel Carl Solander by permission Linnean Society, Joseph Banks NMM: p22-23 photo John Longley, Buchan drawing & James Cook chart by permission of the British Library: p24 photos left & inset John Longley, painting Pickersgill Harbour NMM: p25 photo by kind permission Cary Wolinsky (NGS), Cook's chart New Zealand by permission of the British Library: p26-27 photos by kind permission David Doubilet (National Geographic Society), inset engraving NMM, Cook's chart Botany Bay by permission British Library, Parkinson painting Natural History Museum: p28 NMM: p29 Munkhouse portrait by permission Christie's Images, painting NMM: p30 photo Joe Tyrrell: p31 picture by John Webber NMM.

Thanks to Jenny Longley, Jacky Law, Zoe Hardie-Lyddon and Carol Sandford for proof reading and comments.

A CIP Catalogue for this book is available from the British Library. ISBN 1 86007 051 5.

The above map shows Captain Cook's three voyages around the world

Deptford Yard to Board of Admiralty March 1768

"The Earl of Pembroke, Mr Thos Milner, owner, was built at Whitby, her age three years nine months, square stern bark, single bottom, full built and comes nearest to the tonnage mentioned in your warrant and not so old by fourteen months, is a promising ship for sailing of this kind and fit to stow provisions and stores as may be put on board her."

Navy Board Warrant April 1768

"Ship purchased to be sheathed, filled and fitted for a voyage to the southward. To be called the Endeavour"

James Cook 1771

"No Sea can hurt her laying Too under a Main Sail or Mizon ballanc'd"

ISBN 1860070515

9 781860 070518

Financial Options

By M Desmond Fitzgerald

Euromoney Publications